halloween treats

halloween treats

recipes and crafts for the whole family

by donata maggipinto

photographs by richard jung

CHRONICLE BOOKS

SAN FRANCISCO

Chex is a registered trademark of General Mills. X-Acto is a registered trademark of Hunt Manufacturing Co. Spicy Hot V-8 is a registered trademark of Campbell Soup Co. Tabasco is a registered trademark of McIlhenny Co. Marshmallow Fluff is a registered trademark of Durkee-Mower Inc. Jell-O is a registered trademark of Kraft Foods, Inc. Red-Hots by Ferrara Pan is a registered trademark of Candy Co. Jolly Ranchers is a registered trademark of Hershey Foods Corp. LifeSavers is a registered trademark of Nabisco Inc.

Library of Congress Cataloging-in-Publication Data:

Maggipinto, Donata.
    Halloween treats : recipes and crafts for the whole family / by Donata Maggipinto.
        p.   cm.
    ISBN 0-8118-2197-8
    1. Halloween cookery. 2. Halloween decorations. I. Title.
TX739.2.H34M34   1998
641.5'68—dc21   98-4547
                    CIP

Printed in Hong Kong.

Design and illustration by Carrie Leeb, Leeb & Sons
Prop styling by Carole Hacker
Food styling by Pouké
Crafts by Michelle Syracuse

Distributed in Canada by Raincoast Books
8680 Cambie Street, Vancouver, British Columbia V6P 6M9

10 9 8 7 6 5 4 3 2 1

Chronicle Books
85 Second Street, San Francisco, California 94105

www.chroniclebooks.com

The photographer wishes to thank Donata for her enthusiasm and creative input, Pouké for her inspiring creativity, Michelle Syracuse for her commitment to quality, Ivy for her relentless attention to detail, Carole Hacker for knowing what I like and where to get it, and my wife and daughter for being my most valued critics and advisors. Thanks also to Leslie Jonath, Pamela Geismar, and Erica Jacobs, at Chronicle Books for their support and hard work.

Carole Hacker would like to thank Naomi's of San Francisco, 1817 Polk Street, 415.775.1207.

To Kate and Evan Tavera, my favorite pixies.

The idea for this book was sprouted by Victoria Kalish, book buyer for Williams-Sonoma, and I thank her for leading me down this enchanted path.

To everyone at Chronicle Books for literally working magic to create this book on time. Many thanks to my editor, Leslie Jonath, for her enthusiasm, able guidance, and willingness to jump headlong into the world of Halloween tricks and treats. A ditto on that sentiment to Erica Jacobs and an additional thanks for her buy-in to my "have fun" philosophy. Thanks to Pamela Geismar and her great design staff for their creative vision. I am grateful to Sharon Silva for her keen eye and astute observations, and to Mikyla Bruder for keeping everybody and everything in sync.

I owe special gratitude to my crack photography team, who dove in with enthusiasm and the usual esprit de corps. Thanks to Richard Jung for his creative eye and technical talent; each photo is a charm. Kisses to Pouké for her food artistry and sense of whimsy. A very special thank you to Michelle Syracuse, who interpreted the crafts with style and a healthy dose of fun. Hugs to Carole Hacker for her uncanny ability to unearth perfect props. And big thanks to the industrious, intuitive, and inventive Lissa Ivy.

As always, I send all my love and thanks to Courtney Reeser, who, in addition to offering such crucial Halloween input as "spiders have 8 legs, not 6" (who knew?), also provided me with the patience, encouragement, and good humor that helped this book come to life.

A big hug to Angela Miller for her solid advice and loyal support.

Many, many thanks to my family, friends, and associates for listening to my hare-brained ideas with a straight face and for their generous support at every turn.

I must send my gratitude to elementary school teachers everywhere without whose inventiveness and creativity when it comes to Halloween crafts I would have no memories of Kleenex-and-cotton ball ghosts and paper bag pumpkins and, hence, no inspiration for this book.

table of contents

happy halloween!

When the night air turns spine-chilling and autumn leaves crackle under our feet, we know that Halloween will be whistling in soon. Nothing is quite what it seems. A ghost flies by—or is it just a sheet hanging on the clothesline? A bat hovers in a tree—or is it only a bird? Children become grown-ups and adults become children.

Halloween confirms what children have known all along: playing dress-up and eating sweets is a fantastical route to a magical world. While most of our lives are spent adhering to others' notions of being grown-up, Halloween bestows no-holds-barred permission to masquerade as whatever or whomever we please. And with luscious treats and fanciful adornments at its heart, who wouldn't be impatient for its arrival?

The holiday as we know it sprang from a bubbling cauldron of rituals and beliefs born two thousand years ago with the Celtic harvest festivals in Great Britain and Ireland. While the Celts celebrated the bounty of the season, they also faced the upcoming dark days of winter with apprehension. With the waning of the festival's daylight hours came the inky night known as All Hallows' Eve, or Halloween. A hallow is the spirit of a dead person or saint, and it was believed that on this night spirits were allowed to roam freely.

Festooning themselves in costumes and masks so the spirits wouldn't recognize them, the Celts offered sweets called soul cakes in exchange for deliverance from evil tricks. They carved turnips and beets and placed candles in them in the belief that the light would keep the spirits at bay.

When the Irish immigrated to America in the 1800s, the more superstitious and impish aspects of Halloween were embraced by the Victorians, who harbored a fascination with magic and a penchant for mischievous frolic. In its American interpretation, Halloween was transformed from a chilling ritual provoked by fright to a holiday of ghoulish glee stirred by a desire for fun.

Turnips and beets were replaced by the pumpkin, native to America, and jack-o'-lanterns smiled toothily or leered ghoulishly from porches and windowsills as decorative send-offs to the holiday. Groups of revelers toured neighborhoods in the same spirit as Christmas carolers, and were rewarded with treats for their creative costumes.

Halloween has become one of America's most popular holidays, enjoyed by kids and adults alike. It's a great time to cook and decorate, to eat and celebrate. In fact, getting ready for Halloween can be as much fun as the eve itself, and it presents a wonderful opportunity for spending time with friends and family and, of course, with our favorite sprites—our kids.

how to use this book

The recipes and crafts in this book are definitely doable without a major outlay of time or money. They're designed to delight both children and adults, but adults are clearly at the helm when it comes to organizing and supervising the Halloween activities. It's about working together and having fun while you chop, stir, cut, and paste.

Sometimes, though, there is nothing I want more than to hole up in the kitchen with a good idea and a great-tasting recipe and work my own magic for the benefit of adult friends or family members. Therefore, I have included a few adult Halloween pleasures as well, such as a sophisticated Halloween dinner party.

Throughout the book, you will discover many ways to involve, inspire, and excite your children (and yourself, too!). The recipes will enable kids to learn basic cooking skills such as chopping, measuring, and sautéing. There is something for everyone to do, from the curious four-year-old to the young teenager. The tasks increase in interest with the age of the child, and adults should assign activities based on a child's experience and maturity.

The pixies, children aged four to eight, can chop softer vegetables, fruits, and cheese with a plastic knife and stir with a plastic spoon. They can add ingredients as you read the recipe aloud. (Have on hand a step stool so your pixies can have a good view of what's going on in the bowl or the pot.) This is a great opportunity for your little ones to learn life skills, such as counting, measuring, and listening, and to experience the world with all their senses, as they see, smell, hear, feel, and taste the wonders of cooking.

Older and more experienced children can use a paring knife under your supervision. Let them read the recipe with you and follow the directions, such as "add ½ teaspoon salt" or "beat until light and fluffy." Assign them the important job of taste tester, and allow them to decide if the dish you're cooking needs more salt or pepper or sugar. They'll exercise their budding proficiency in math, reading, and vocabulary; experience the magic of culinary chemistry as they watch how ingredients work together; and earn the satisfaction of seeing a project through from start to finish.

Creating crafts is a lot like cooking, and many of the same learning opportunities exist. Children aged four to eight will delight in the Pixie Projects, creative tasks that allow them to color, glue, cut out shapes and paint with fingers, brushes, and sponges. You can make it easier and safer for them by supplying child-friendly materials such as blunt-tip scissors and nontoxic—and washable—paints and markers, and by gently guiding them through the projects. Older children can draw freehand or trace, cut with scissors, carve pumpkins (with adult supervision), paint, weave fabric, sew, and piece together diverse components to make artful objects.

Whenever I approach any celebration, my mind naturally categorizes and organizes, particularly if children are involved in the preparations. Following this inclination, I have divided the book into three sections: First comes Halloween Anticipations, which includes recipes for snack treats and a Halloween lunch box and instructions for making a Halloween trick-or-treat basket and bag, as well as a candy bowl for handing out the treats! The second section, Halloween Enchantments, serves up cauldron or one-dish recipes, as well as side dishes and a dessert that will embellish a Halloween dinner party. Assorted crafts are interspersed throughout the section, among them ideas for adding a seasonable ambience to your home and table and kids' projects guaranteed to bring them ghoulish glee! Finally, Halloween Excitements delivers a bundle of recipes for toothsome goodies plus a wealth of ideas for making fun things to decorate.

Your little ones will jump into the Pixie Projects found throughout the book and will enjoy helping you toast pumpkin seeds or make marshmallow ghosts for hot cocoa. Older kids can stretch their Halloween imaginations with crafts that use natural elements to create fanciful decorations, and will leap into preparing (and eating) seasonal treats like caramel Lady apples and Pumpkin Pie Ice Cream. And for anyone who can't resist hosting a Halloween dinner party, I have included a menu for an adult gathering and ideas for creating a whimsical yet stylish holiday table.

Follow the directions to the letter and you'll come up with some deliciously fun treats and Halloween embellishments. But I hope that you'll regard the instructions as a guide and let your imagination take you for a spin.

Children are inherently creative and naturally curious. They flourish when they can express their original ideas in a caring and open environment—an environment in which their individuality and the creativity that springs from it—is treasured. As adults, our role is that of caretaker, teacher, and guide—with a healthy dose of unabashed adoration thrown in.

Adopt my Halloween credo and approach this book in the spirit in which it was written—with fun, frolic, and a little bit of good-natured fright.

Happy Halloween!

kid tips for cooking and crafting

Cooking and crafting are a lot of fun, but sometimes they can be dangerous, particularly when a group is involved. Potential rough spots can be smoothed out in advance, however, if you outline responsibilities and discuss safety before you begin. Here are a few tips that will help you and your kids cook and craft in ways that are both safe and fun. You may want to pass this on to an older child who can read it aloud.

before you begin...

get yourself ready:

* Tie back long hair and protect your clothes with a smock or apron. Wash your hands thoroughly with soap and water.

prepare your work area:

* Read through the entire recipe or the craft instructions and collect all the ingredients and equipment you will need.

* Determine who will do which tasks.

* Make sure you know how all tools and appliances operate.

* If you're doing a craft, cover the work area with newspaper.

while you're cooking or crafting:

* Clean as you go; you'll be more efficient and the cleanup will be easier.

* Keep everything except what's actually cooking away from the hot stovetop.

* Never use wet hands to turn on a light switch or to pull out or push in a plug.

* Use sharp tools such as knives and scissors with extreme care (children will need adult assistance). When you're not using the tools, put them in a safe place so nobody gets hurt.

when you're finished:

* Clean up and put all equipment and ingredients away. Give yourself a pat on the back for a job well done!

special cooking tips:

These are familiar rules, but they bear repeating, particularly if you're cooking with children.

* Turn pot handles away from the edge of the stove so nobody passing by bumps into them.

* Don't leave metal utensils inside pots on the stovetop or in the oven. Metal is an efficient heat conductor.

* Don't use wet potholders or dishtowels to lift hot pots or dishes. The heat will travel right through the wetness and burn your hand.

* Always lift a pot lid away from you at an angle, so the hot steam does not rise into your face.

* Turn off the stove or oven before removing anything from it.

* Never put metal in a microwave; use only microwave-safe dishes.

* Be careful when you remove food from the microwave, especially if it's covered with plastic wrap, which traps steam that can burn you.

* Always wash your hands and utensils and cutting boards after handling food, especially raw meat, poultry, or seafood.

working with knives and other sharp tools

* Carry knives and scissors with their points facing down.

* Don't cut up food held in your hand. Always put the food on a cutting board.

* Hold knives and scissors with a solid grip and keep your fingers away from the blades.

* Keep sharp tools stored in a safe place until you're ready to use them. Put them away as soon as you have finished with them.

* Wash sharp tools one at a time. Don't put them in soapy water until you're ready to wash them, or somebody may reach into the water and get cut.

halloween anticipations

recipes and crafts for pre-halloween fun

roasted pumpkin seeds

2 cups pumpkin seeds

2 tablespoons vegetable oil

1 teaspoon salt, or more to taste

I don't know which is more fun, carving Jack or roasting the seeds. One 4-pound pumpkin will yield about 2 cups seeds. Save the seeds whenever you carve a pumpkin (page 26), then roast some of them and plant some of them. Next year, you'll have your own pumpkin patch—and lots of roasted pumpkin seeds! Kids and pixies can stir and toss the seeds with salt or spices and help spread them on the baking sheet.

Makes 2 cups

Preheat an oven to 350° F.

Rinse the seeds well in cold water, being sure you have rinsed away any fibrous strings, and pat thoroughly dry. Transfer to a large bowl and add the vegetable oil and salt, stirring well to coat the seeds with the oil. Spread the seeds on a baking sheet in a single layer. Bake until crisp and golden, 12 to 15 minutes. Taste for seasoning and add more salt if desired.

variations

* Herbed Seeds: Use olive oil in place of the vegetable oil and add 1 tablespoon each dried rosemary and dried basil along with the salt.

* Spicy Seeds: Add 2 teaspoons chili powder along with the salt.

* Indian Seeds: Add 1½ tablespoons curry powder and a pinch of cayenne pepper along with the salt.

* Pumpkin Pie Seeds: Substitute 4 tablespoons (½ stick) melted butter for the vegetable oil and add 3 tablespoons light brown sugar, 1½ teaspoons ground cinnamon, ½ teaspoon ground allspice, and a pinch each of ground nutmeg, ground cloves, and salt.

halloween crunch mix

A spooky rendition of the perennially popular "party mix," this recipe makes lots of the crunchy, salty-sweet snack. The best way to mix this is with your hands—and kids will adore being assigned this task. Store the leftovers in an airtight tin for up to 3 weeks.

Makes 6 cups

Combine all the ingredients in a large bowl and mix well. Dive in!

1 cup Roasted Pumpkin Seeds (see recipe on page 18)

1 cup dried cranberries

1 cup candy corn

1 cup roasted peanuts

1 cup corn cereal such as Chex

1 cup pretzel sticks

maple cider punch

Whip up a batch of citrusy, sparkly punch for sipping while carving jack-o'-lanterns. Make a toast to the fun and frolic of Halloween. Kids can help measure and stir the ingredients.

Makes 6 servings

Pour the orange juice into a small saucepan, and stir in the maple syrup. Place over medium heat and bring almost to a boil. Remove from the heat, stir once or twice, and let cool to room temperature. (Or combine the orange juice and maple syrup in a microwave-safe bowl and microwave on high for 3 minutes.)

Pour the apple cider into a pitcher and add the cooled orange juice and the ginger ale. Mix well. Serve over ice.

1 cup orange juice

3 tablespoons maple syrup

4 cups apple cider, chilled

1 cup ginger ale, chilled

ice cubes

baked sweet potato chips

4–6 tablespoons vegetable oil

6 sweet potatoes, unpeeled

salt to taste

Low in fat and high in flavor, baked sweet potato chips will satisfy hunger pangs during Halloween activities. Kids can help toss the chips with the oil and spread them on the baking sheets. Try this recipe with parsnips and beets, too.

Makes 6 servings

Preheat an oven to 400° F. Set aside 2 nonstick baking sheets or lightly brush 2 regular baking sheets with some of the vegetable oil.

Using the slicing disk of a food processor, or a mandoline or sharp knife, cut the sweet potatoes into ⅛-inch slices. Put the remaining vegetable oil in a large bowl, add the sweet potatoes, and toss to coat with the oil. Season with salt.

Spread the potato slices on the baking sheets in a single layer (you may have to do this in batches). Bake, turning once, until crisp and golden, 15 to 17 minutes.

Remove from the oven and transfer to paper towels to drain. Add more salt, if desired. Serve immediately, or store in airtight tins for up to 1 week.

hot cocoa with marshmallow spooks

Nothing beats a cup of hot cocoa after an afternoon spent jumping into piles of autumn leaves. The marshmallow spooks make terrific (or is it terror-ific?) toppers. Let the kids roll and stamp out the marshmallow spooks with mini cookie cutters.

Makes 6 cups

Place 1 marshmallow horizontally on a work surface. Using a rolling pin or soup can, flatten the marshmallow by rolling back and forth over it. Using Halloween-themed mini cookie cutters, cut into desired shapes.

In a saucepan over medium heat, combine the cocoa, sugar, and water. Bring slowly to a boil, stirring, until the sugar and cocoa dissolve, about 2 minutes. Add the milk and half-and-half and continue to cook, stirring, until bubbles appear along the edges of the pan, about 5 minutes; do not allow to boil. Pour into mugs and garnish with the marshmallow spooks. Serve immediately while the spooks hold their shapes.

6 to 8 large marshmallows

5 tablespoons unsweetened Dutch-process cocoa

3 tablespoons sugar

1/3 cup water

4 cups milk

1 cup half-and-half

halloween lunch box

A Halloween-themed lunch will add ghoulish gaiety to your child's day (or your husband's or wife's, for that matter). Pack all the treats in a paper bag and print the word Boo on the front in black tempera paint.

ghost-wiches

Using a cookie cutter (or do it freehand), cut bread into ghost shapes. Cut out O's for the eyes and mouth with the point of a pastry tip or plastic condiment bottle. Spread the ghostly bread slices with peanut butter and jelly, or if you're really ambitious, use the same cookie cutter to cut your child's favorite luncheon meats and cheeses into spooky shapes.

apple jack-o'-lanterns

Choose an apple with a stem, and slice off its top to form a jack-o'-lantern lid. Using an apple corer, carefully remove the core to within $\frac{1}{2}$-inch of the blossom end. With a melon baller or a sharp-edged spoon, hollow out the whole apple, leaving a $\frac{1}{2}$-inch-thick shell. With a paring knife, cut out the eyes and mouth. Rub all the cut surfaces with a lemon wedge to prevent browning. Fill the apple jack-o'-lantern with raisins or dried fruits, replace the lid, and wrap well in plastic wrap.

witch's hair and goblin's eyeballs

Peel and shred 2 carrots, and peel 6 seedless grapes. Combine the carrots and grapes in a bowl, add your child's favorite salad dressing, and toss well. Spoon into a small plastic container with a tight-fitting top, and pack a plastic spoon.

be a good ghoul at
school and you will get
a surprise! your favorite
rat tail soup
and spider
dessert

and dea

Along with the lunch treats, tuck into the bag a slip of paper on which you've written a Halloween joke ("What is a ghost's favorite food?" "Boo-berries!") or fortune ("A black cat will cross your path!").

how to carve a jack-o'-lantern

What image comes to your mind when I say "Halloween?" Bet you answered "pumpkin!" This roly-poly, jolly orange squash is the unofficial mascot of the season. Festivals celebrate it. Gardeners grow it. Contests weigh it. Cooks bake it. Even Cinderella knew a good thing when she saw it—she hitched a ride in it! But carving the pumpkin into a Halloween luminary is a ritual unto itself.

Kids love to make jack-o'-lanterns, but they need lots of adult assistance. As carving a pumpkin can be unwieldy at times, this task is best left to an adult. Kids can get into the act by drawing the jack-o'-lantern's face and helping to scoop out the pumpkin's flesh and seeds. Here are some tips for carving Jack with safety and success:

first things first

* Choose a firm pumpkin free of bruises or cuts.

* Line a large work area with newspaper. If the weather is good, this is an ideal outdoor project.

* Lay out your equipment and supplies: small, sharp knife; thin serrated knife (an X-Acto blade is best); long-handled spoon; large bowl filled with water (for seeds); paper and pencils (for drawing faces and or patterns); masking tape; pushpins; flour (to highlight the design);

paper towels; garbage bag; votive candle; metal jar lid or saucer to hold the candle; long matches.

make a star-quality lid

Draw a star around the stem. Using the small, sharp knife, cut it out, angling the cut inward as you do to form a natural ledge on which the lid can rest.

get rid of the goop!

Scoop out the seeds and strings, and scrape the insides of the pumpkin to release the fibers. Your hands work best for the scooping, and the spoon or a butter curler (really!) works best for the scraping. Transfer the seeds to a bowl of cold water and save for roasting.

be an artist

* On a sheet of paper, draw a face (scary or happy, funny or sad), a pattern (harlequin, spirals, or stripes), a Halloween icon (cat, ghost, or witch), or a greeting (boo! beware! or Happy Halloween).

* Align your design on the pumpkin, and secure it with the masking tape.

trace, poke, cut

* Using a pushpin, trace your design in a series of pricks about $\frac{1}{8}$-inch apart. It's not necessary to push the pin all the way through the pumpkin. Just pierce the surface so you can see the design when the paper is lifted.

* Remove the paper. If you have trouble seeing your pattern, dust it with flour.

* Using the thin, serrated knife or X-Acto blade, cut along your pattern from dot to dot. For this step, you *do* want to push all the way through the pumpkin. Take your time. This is a slow process, but worthwhile in the end!

* Use the eraser end of a pencil to poke out sticking pieces.

let there be candlelight

* Rest the upturned metal jar lid or saucer on the "floor" of the pumpkin, and place the votive candle on it.

* Tip the pumpkin slightly and carefully light the candle.

* Replace the pumpkin lid for a few moments, then lift it and note where the candle smoke has left a mark. Cut a hole 1 inch in diameter at the spot to function as a chimney.

say jack-o'-lantern!

* Take a picture of your child posing with the jack-o'-lantern and send it to Grandma or a friend.

how to carve squash-o'-lanterns

A jack-o'-lantern is nothing more than a decked-out squash, so why not gild his relatives, too? The big, blue Hubbard, the slender, beige butternut, the exotic turban, the pale and elegant cheese pumpkin—each will blossom in its own special way once decorated for the occasion.

Follow the carving instructions for the jack-o'-lantern, but bear in mind that some squash varieties have thicker skins than others and will demand more patience. For example, stay away from gourds. Their exceptionally tough skins call for an artist blessed with bucketfuls of perseverance and time.

Unlike pumpkins with their flat tops, many squashes have rounded and pointed crowns that are best left intact. Instead of carving a lid in the top of the squash, cut a hole in the bottom. To light the squash-o'-lantern, place the votive candle on an upturned metal jar lid. Light the candle, then place the squash-o'-lantern over it.

how to carve hanging squash-o'-lanterns

* Select small squashes or root vegetables such as turnips or acorn squashes.

* Cut off the tops and discard.

* Scoop out any seeds, then, using a small ice cream scoop or a melon baller, hollow out the insides, leaving a shell at least a $\frac{1}{4}$-inch thick.

* Draw a face with a light-colored felt-tipped pen. Using a thin, sharp knife (an X-Acto knife is best), cut out the face.

* Using a metal skewer, pierce a small hole on each side of the face, toward the top. Thread a piece of twine or leather, cut to the desired length, through the holes and knot each end from the inside to secure it.

* Lay a small piece of aluminum foil on the bottom of the squash. Place a votive candle on it, and carefully light it.

* Hang the squash-'o-lanterns from tree branches or lamp posts or secure along a clothesline. For indoor decoration, parade them along a fireplace mantle.

trick-or-treat bag

A run-of-the-mill paper grocery bag is transformed into a fanciful Halloween treat bag with the help of rubber stamps, stickers, and, if you please, a glitter pen. Let your imagination run wild when you decorate—the scarier, the merrier! Pixies will need help folding and hole-punching the bag.

Fold down the top of the bag three times, making a sturdy two-inch-wide band. Punch 2 holes, one at each end, into the band. Adults can reinforce the bag by using the clear nail polish to paint a 1/4-inch-wide border around the holes, both inside and outside the bag.

Using rubber stamps, stickers, and if you like, a glitter pen, decorate the bag. Let the ink dry. Thread the twine, leather, or ribbon through the holes in the band, then tie to secure, forming a handle.

For each bag you will need:

1 large grocery bag, preferably without graphics

1/8-inch-hole paper punch

clear nail polish (optional)

rubber stamps and inks

stickers

glitter pen (optional)

18-inch-length twine, leather, or ribbon

indian corn bracelets

For each bracelet you will need:

Indian corn kernels

heavy elastic thread

embroidery needle

This natural bracelet will delight both girls and boys. Intersperse the corn kernels with beads if you want to be showy. Pixies should not use the needle without adult supervision.

Put the corn kernels in a bowl and cover with hot water. Let stand overnight. Drain.

Cut the thread to the desired length (big enough so that once the ends are tied, your child's hand will still fit through) and knot one end. Thread the needle with the unknotted end. String the corn kernels onto the thread. Tie the ends together. Let dry overnight.

trick-or-treat basket

For each basket you will need:

construction paper

metallic pens

glitter

craft glue

1 basket or box (available at art supply or craft stores)

decorative cord or ribbon

Explore art supply or craft stores for a ready-made basket, then embellish it to your heart's content. Kids can help with all aspects of the decorating process—and they'll adore having their name personalizing their treat basket.

Draw and cut Halloween motifs, and your child's name if desired, from the construction paper. Decorate the cut-outs with the metallic pens and glitter. Glue the cut-outs to the basket. Thread the cord or ribbon through the basket to form a handle.

flying ghosts

Perception is reality in the case of flying ghosts. Clear monofilament is invisible from a few steps away, so when you use it to hang the ghosts, they really look like they're flying. Only you and your pixie will know the secret. Your pixie may need help cutting the fabric and tying the ghosts.

Place the screen on a flat surface and spray generously with spray adhesive. Carefully lay the tissue paper on the screen and using the palms of your hands, smooth it of any wrinkles.

To form the head of the ghost, form a fist with your hand and place the screen over it. Using your free hand, mold the screen over your fist. Remove your hand and with both hands, mold the screen to form the arms and ghost body. Decorate with sequins, rhinestones, wiggle-eyes and/or buttons.

Thread the monofilament through the needle, knot one end, and thread it from the inside of the ghost out through the top of the head. Hang the ghost from a light fixture, tree branch, or a hook in a doorway and watch it fly!

For each ghost you will need:

fine mesh screen, 15-inch square

spray mount adhesive (available at art supply stores)

white tissue paper, 17-inch square

craft glue

sequins, rhinestones, wiggle eyes, and/or buttons, for decorating

clear monofilament (available at sporting goods stores)

sewing needle

papier-mâché jack-o'-lantern candy bowl

For each candy bowl you will need:

1 large mixing bowl, taller than it is wide

petroleum jelly

newspapers

1 cup wheat paste or wallpaper paste

orange and black tempera paints

Papier-mâché is one of the great inventions. Flour, water, and newspapers are transformed into shapes and illusions, and all we have to do is get our hands messy! You can find wheat paste and wallpaper paste at craft, hardware, and do-it-yourself home stores, or you can make your own papier-mâché paste following your favorite recipe.

Grease the exterior of the bowl with petroleum jelly, coating the bottom and sides completely. Cut the newspapers into long 1½-inch-wide strips.

In another large bowl, mix the paste with enough warm water to create a thin, creamy solution. Dip the newspaper strips into the paste, a few at a time, to moisten them, and cover the bowl with 2 layers of wet strips. Leave a 1-inch border uncovered around the top of the bowl so you can free it once the papier-mâché has dried. Let dry fully, then apply 2 more layers of newspaper strips to the bowl. Let dry again, then repeat the process one more time. Let dry overnight.

The next day, dislodge the bowl and pull it out. Pixies can help you finish the project. Paint the papier-mâché with orange tempera paint and let dry. Paint the jack-o'-lantern's features with the black tempera paint and let dry completely. Now fill with treats!

more ideas for candy cauldrons

The vessel from which you hand out Halloween candy doesn't need to be a bowl. Think scary or whimsical or funny, and tickle your guests' fancies when you offer them their treats.

* Scout flea markets and secondhand stores for a cast-iron kettle with

a looped handle. This rendition of a witch's cauldron will delight young guests (not to mention give your arms a workout).

∗ Turn a witch's hat (available at most costume stores) upside down and fill it with treats.

∗ Wrap a tin bucket with black and orange crepe paper.

∗ Hollow out a pumpkin and drop in a plastic bowl for holding the candy.

∗ Transform an empty fish bowl into a Halloween treat bowl.

∗ Purchase a rubber witch's hand from a costume store, then wear it when you dip your hand into the candy bowl and offer treats to your Halloween guests.

halloween hand warmers

For each pair of hand warmers you will need:

1 pair of cotton or wool mittens or gloves (the flatter and less fuzzy the surface, the better)

1 piece of cardboard, large enough to accommodate both mittens or gloves laid flat for tracing

fabric paint in nozzle bottles

In many parts of the country, Halloween ushers in spine-tingling shivers of a different sort—cold weather! Fabric paint and a bit of imagination transform mittens or gloves into Halloween hand warmers for accepting treats with style. Have your pixie help decorate their own mittens.

Place the mittens or gloves flat on the cardboard. Trace their outlines, then cut out the silhouettes. Insert them into the mittens or gloves. Paint Halloween designs on the mittens or gloves and let dry overnight.

Remove the cardboard silhouettes, slip in small hands and head out the door!

leaf lanterns

Line up these translucent lanterns along a table, or use them to light a path to your door on Halloween night. Older children can handle this project from start to finish; pixies will enjoy collecting colorful autumn leaves.

Place 1 piece of waxed paper on a work surface with the waxy side facing up. Arrange leaves on top, spacing them at least 1 inch apart. Put the second piece of waxed paper on top of the leaves with the waxy side facing down. Cover the layered paper with the tea towel or pressing cloth and, using the iron on a low setting, press carefully until the wax melts and secures the leaves.

Fold the fabric strips in half lengthwise and iron them to form a crease. Insert the long edges of the waxed paper into the fabric fold and glue to secure in place. Form into a cylinder and staple or glue the ends of each fabric strip.

Place a votive candle in a votive candle holder, light the candle, and place the lantern over it. *(For photo of leaf lantern, see page 44.)*

For each lantern you will need:

two 6-by-12-inch pieces of waxed paper

selection of colorful autumn leaves

tea towel or pressing cloth

iron

two 2-by-12-inch strips of grosgrain ribbon or cotton fabric, solid or patterned in brown, orange, or red tones

fabric glue

votive candle

votive candle holder

leaf rubbings

This is a great field-trip project. Pack your supplies in a backpack and search for leaves "in the wild," which may be as close as your local park. Or visit a graveyard to make grave rubbings. Look for the oldest graves and the funniest names you can find.

Look for leaves with pronounced veining. Set the leaf on a flat surface. Place the paper on top of the leaf and rub hard with the chalk, pencil, or charcoal. If you wish, cut out the leaf and hang it on the refrigerator or a bulletin board.

You will need:

selection of autumn leaves

tracing paper

colored chalk, pencils, artists' charcoal (available at art supply or craft stores)

fanciful masks

Dime-store masks take on fanciful personalities (as do the people who wear them) when decorated with seasonal items and natural finds. Pixies can create simple collage masks while older children (including adults) can create more sophisticated masks like the ones shown in the photograph.

possible decorations:

small colorful autumn leaves (collect them at least 1 week prior to making the mask); wax or paper wrappers from bite-size candies such as Tootsie Rolls and Mary Janes, twisted in the center to form a bow; stickers; Indian corn or colored popcorn (unpopped); sequins; feathers; fabric trim such as pom-poms.

Have the mask ready, along with the objects that you are using to decorate the mask. Working with one decoration at a time, spread glue onto the back and arrange on the mask. Begin at the outer edge of the mask and work inward, covering the surface completely. When you get to the eye holes, either fold the edges of the flat objects toward the back of the mask or trim them. Let the mask dry completely before wearing.

For each mask you will need:

a plain dime-store mask, white or black

clear-drying craft glue

41

flashlight lanterns

For each flashlight lantern you will need:

lamp shade paper (available at art supply stores)

pencil or felt-tip pen

X-Acto knife

black tempera paint

craft glue

orange or yellow tissue paper

duct tape for securing the shade, if needed

A small lamp shade paper cone can transform an everyday flashlight into a Halloween-night torchère. Bring your flashlight to the art supply store when purchasing the lamp shade paper, so you can size it to fit. Slip it, handle first, through the interior of the lamp shade. The shade should stop naturally when the head of the flashlight touches the opening at the top.

Form the lamp shade paper into a cone shape to fit around the head of the flashlight; cut off the excess paper.

Using a pencil or felt-tip pen, draw scary figures, such as witches, ghosts, and bats, on the outside of the lamp shade. Cut them out with the X-Acto knife. Paint one side of the lamp shade paper black and let dry. Glue tissue paper to the unpainted interior of the lamp shade paper to cover the cutouts.

Place the lamp shade cone over the flashlight and glue (or staple) the seams. Secure in place inside with the duct tape. (A tip: wrap 2 pieces of duct tape around the neck of the flashlight and tape the ends to the inside of the lamp shade.)

halloween enchantments

food from the cauldron, menu for a halloween dinner party, and crafts for dressing up halloween

roasted autumn vegetables with herbed couscous

For the vegetables:

¼ cup olive oil

4 carrots, peeled and cut into 2-inch chunks

2 small rutabagas, peeled and cut into 1-inch chunks

2 parsnips, peeled and cut into 2-inch chunks

6 small new potatoes, unpeeled, halved

½ small butternut squash, peeled, seeded, and cut into 1-inch chunks

6 cloves garlic, unpeeled

4 sprigs fresh rosemary, each 2 inches long

2 tablespoons balsamic vinegar

salt and ground pepper to taste

For the couscous:

6 cups chicken broth

3 cups instant couscous

1 tablespoon grated orange zest

1 tablespoon chopped fresh rosemary

1 tablespoon chopped fresh parsley

1 tablespoon walnut oil

salt and ground pepper to taste

Couscous is nothing more than pasta, so chances are good that your children will give it a thumbs-up. Maybe they'll like it so much they won't notice the vegetables (maybe when Halloween witches can't fly). If not, you can serve them the couscous on its own. You can omit the orange zest, herbs, and walnut oil from the couscous and add 3 to 4 tablespoons of butter in their place. Feel free to vary the vegetable selection based on your preference. Have your kids help you choose the vegetables.

Serves 6

Preheat an oven to 425° F. Lightly brush a shallow roasting pan with some of the olive oil.

Combine all the vegetables, the garlic, and the rosemary sprigs in a large bowl. Add the remaining oil and the vinegar and toss to coat the vegetables and herb sprigs evenly. Season with salt and pepper and transfer to the prepared roasting pan. Roast until the vegetables are tender when pierced with a fork, about 45 minutes.

When the vegetables are about half cooked, make the couscous. Place the broth in a saucepan and bring to a boil. Stir in the couscous, remove from the heat, cover, and let stand for 15 minutes. Gently mix in the orange zest, rosemary, parsley, and walnut oil, fluffing the couscous with a fork. Season with salt and pepper.

Remove the vegetables from the oven, and retrieve the garlic cloves from the pan. To serve, spoon the couscous onto warmed plates and top with the roasted vegetables. Squeeze a garlic clove over each serving to free the pungent pulp from its papery skin. The mildly flavored roasted garlic paste is an ideal condiment for mixing into the vegetables and couscous.

deviled ham

Any bit of piquancy can earn a dish the label "deviled." In this spread for crackers or sandwiches, a double dose of mustard definitely lends a devilish bite. If your audience includes kids, you may want to mellow the spread by eliminating the mustard and cloves and adding another tablespoon of sweet relish.

Makes about 2 cups

In a food processor, combine the ham, Dijon mustard, dry mustard, butter, mayonnaise, and the cloves, if using. Puree coarsely. Transfer to a bowl and stir in the onion, relish, salt and pepper. Cover and chill well before serving.

¾ pound cooked ham, cut into 1-inch pieces

2 tablespoons Dijon mustard

2 teaspoons English-style dry mustard

2 tablespoons (¼ stick) unsalted butter, softened

1 tablespoon mayonnaise

pinch of ground cloves (optional)

3 tablespoons grated onion

3 tablespoons sweet relish

salt and pepper to taste

corn-print place mats

Ears of corn, dried or fresh, offer a ready-made pattern for printing place mats (and napkins and tablecloths). Other vegetables and fruits that are ripe for printing include sliced mushrooms, potatoes (carve a design into the flesh), and halved apples and lemons. To make it easier for little hands, insert corn picks in either end of the corn.

Pour the fabric paint into a shallow pan. Roll the ½ ear of corn in the paint to coat it, shake off the excess, and roll it along the place mat. Repeat this process until the place mat is decorated to your liking. Let the paint dry completely.

Note: If you'd like to use various paint colors for decorating, either rinse the ½ ear of corn and dry it well before proceeding to the next color, or easier still, assign ½ ear of corn for each color.

For each place mat you will need:

fabric paint

½ ear shucked Indian corn, uncooked

1 cotton place mat, in a light color such as white or yellow

black risotto

6 cups chicken broth

2 tablespoons olive oil

1 onion, chopped

2 cloves garlic, minced

2 cups Arborio rice

½ cup dry red wine

3 tablespoons tapenade or
black olive paste

2 tablespoons chopped fresh
rosemary

2 tablespoons grated orange zest

½ cup freshly grated Parmesan
cheese, plus more to taste

salt and black pepper to taste

The spooky color of this dish will delight the children and the flavor will send shivers down your spine. It's ghoulishly good. For a fanciful finish, use a cookie cutter or a paring knife to cut out spooky shapes from an orange bell pepper and arrange them on the risotto before serving. Kids will have fun (as will you) cutting out the shapes. They can also help with stirring the risotto.

Serves 6

Place the chicken broth in a saucepan and bring to a boil. Reduce the heat to low, cover, and keep at a bare simmer.

In a large sauté pan or flameproof casserole over medium heat, warm the oil. Add the onion and garlic and sauté, stirring often, until translucent, about 5 minutes. Add the rice and cook, stirring, until coated with the oil, about 2 minutes. Add the red wine and cook, stirring, until it is absorbed, about 2 minutes.

Slowly add 1 cup of the hot broth to the rice and cook, stirring constantly, until it is almost entirely absorbed by the rice. Add ½ cup broth and cook, stirring, until absorbed by the rice. Continue in this manner, adding ½ cup broth at a time and stirring constantly, until all but 1 cup of the broth has been added to the rice.

Stir in the tapenade and continue cooking, now adding the broth ¼ cup at a time and stirring constantly, until the rice is al dente (just tender) and slightly creamy. The rice should reach this point after about 25 minutes.

Stir in the rosemary, orange zest, and ¼ cup Parmesan cheese. Taste and adjust the seasoning with salt and pepper. Serve immediately—risotto waits for no one! Pass more Parmesan cheese at the table.

tomato polenta with a selection of sausages

2 tablespoons olive oil

½ onion, finely chopped

2 cups crushed plum (Roma) tomatoes

2 tablespoons tomato paste

1½ tablespoons fresh oregano or 2 teaspoons dried oregano

1 teaspoon fennel seeds

salt and ground pepper to taste

6 cups chicken broth

2 cups coarse cornmeal (polenta)

½ cup freshly grated Parmesan cheese

12 assorted sausages such as spicy Italian pork sausage, mild Italian turkey sausage, chicken-basil sausage, and lamb-garlic sausage

After a day of carving pumpkins or choosing Halloween costumes, my tired soul calls out for something wholesome and savory. Polenta fits the bill. Here, tomatoes lend a pale orange hue in a nod to Halloween. Kids will think the color is neat. This dish is a fine choice on its own (if so, double the recipe), but it's even better when paired with a selection of sausages. Check your local market for interesting flavors. Anything goes—even hot dogs, which will increase the chances of your kids embracing this vibrant dish.

Serves 6

In a skillet over medium heat, warm the olive oil. Add the onion and sauté until soft and translucent, about 5 minutes. Add the crushed tomatoes, tomato paste, oregano, and fennel seeds. Raise the heat to high and cook uncovered, stirring occasionally, until the sauce thickens a bit, about 10 minutes. Season to taste with salt and pepper. Keep warm.

As the sauce cooks, in a saucepan bring the chicken broth to a boil over medium-high heat. Add the cornmeal by scooping it and letting it fall through the fingers of one hand while you whisk with the other hand. Switch to a wooden spoon, reduce the heat to medium-low, and cook the polenta, stirring constantly, until it is creamy and begins to pull away from the sides of the pan, about 20 minutes.

Stir the tomato sauce and Parmesan cheese into the polenta. Season to taste with salt and pepper.

Meanwhile, cook the sausages: prepare a fire in a charcoal grill or preheat a stovetop grill pan over medium-high heat. When the fire is ready or the grill pan is hot, prick the sausages with a fork and grill them until cooked through, 10 to 12 minutes. The timing depends on the variety of sausage.

To serve, spoon the polenta onto individual plates. Cut the sausages in half lengthwise and arrange on top of the polenta.

warm red cabbage slaw with apples

Red cabbage takes on the flavors of fall with the addition of cranberry nectar and apple. Get your kids to try this—its sweetness may win them over. Depending on their age, kids can help prepare the dish by grating the orange zest, measuring the ingredients, and adding the ingredients to the pan.

Serves 6

In a large sauté pan over low heat, fry the bacon, turning as needed until the fat has rendered and the bacon is crisp and brown, about 8 minutes. Using a slotted spoon, transfer the bacon to paper towels to drain; reserve. Pour off all but 2 tablespoons of the bacon fat from the pan.

Add the balsamic vinegar, cranberry nectar, celery seed, and orange zest to the sauté pan, raise the heat to high, and bring to a boil. Reduce the heat to low and add the cabbage, stirring to combine the ingredients. Cook until the cabbage has wilted, about 4 minutes. Add the apple and bacon, stir again, and cook until heated through, about one minute longer. Transfer to a warmed serving dish and serve at once.

½ pound slab bacon, diced

2 tablespoons balsamic vinegar

¼ cup cranberry nectar

1 teaspoon celery seed

1 teaspoon grated orange zest

3 cups shredded red cabbage

1 large red apple, unpeeled, cored, and chopped

curried pumpkin soup

This vibrantly colored, full-flavored soup will satisfy hungry goblins for Halloween and other guests throughout the autumn (it makes a great addition to Thanksgiving dinner, too). Depending upon their ages and tastes, you might want to leave out the curry and Tabasco if you're serving the soup to children. But even without the spicy accents, this soup is a winner—and it's quick to make, too. Be sure you use a good eating pumpkin such as Jack Be Little, Munchkin, or Spookie rather than the roadside pumpkin-patch variety. Both are edible, but the former, available at most supermarkets, has better texture and taste. Butternut squash is an able pinch hitter.

Serves 6

Cut the pumpkin in half through the center and scoop out the seeds and strings (save the seeds for roasting as directed on page 18). Cut away the hard peel and chop the flesh. You should have about 6 cups.

In a large saucepan over medium-low heat, warm the olive oil with the butter. When the butter melts, add the onion and sauté, stirring occasionally, until translucent, 2 to 3 minutes. Add the broth, pumpkin, and potato, raise the heat to high, and bring to a boil. Reduce the heat to low, cover, and simmer until the vegetables are tender, 20 to 25 minutes.

Working in batches, transfer the vegetables with some of the liquid to a food processor or blender and puree until smooth. Return the puree to the saucepan and stir in the orange zest and curry powder. Place over low heat and stir in the cream and the Tabasco, if using. Season with salt and pepper. Heat to serving temperature.

Ladle the soup into warmed bowls or mugs and sprinkle with the pumpkin seeds. Serve at once.

1 pumpkin, 4 to 5 pounds

2 tablespoons olive oil

1 tablespoon unsalted butter

1 onion, finely chopped

5 cups chicken broth

1 baking potato, peeled and chopped

2 teaspoons grated orange zest

1½ teaspoons curry powder

½ cup heavy cream (optional)

dash of Tabasco sauce (optional)

salt and ground pepper to taste

2 tablespoons roasted pumpkin seeds

three-two chili

1/4 cup olive oil

2 large onions, chopped

3 cloves garlic, minced

2 pounds ground turkey

1 pound ground beef chuck

1/4 cup best-quality chili powder

2 tablespoons ground cumin

1 tablespoon dried oregano

1 1/2 teaspoons ground coriander

1/4 teaspoon cayenne pepper

1 tablespoon grated lime zest

1 can (28 ounces) crushed plum (Roma) tomatoes, undrained

1 cup each canned red kidney beans, black beans, and cannellini or other white beans, rinsed and drained

salt and ground pepper to taste

shredded Monterey Jack cheese, sour cream, cubed avocado, and chopped fresh cilantro

The three *stands for three varieties of beans—kidney, black, and cannellini—and the* two *stands for two types of meat—beef and turkey. All together, three plus two equals hearty and good. I like to make a big batch of this chili and freeze some to eat during the hectic days before Thanksgiving. Kids can help with the measuring, mixing, and stirring, and they'll have fun customizing their chili with the garnishes.*

Serves 6

In a large Dutch oven or flameproof casserole over medium-low heat, warm the olive oil. Add the onions and sauté, stirring, until translucent and soft, about 5 minutes. Add the garlic and cook, stirring, for 1 minute. Add the turkey and beef, raise the heat to medium, and cook, stirring and breaking up any big lumps, until the meat is no longer pink, about 10 minutes.

Add the chili powder, cumin, oregano, coriander, cayenne, and lime zest, and cook, stirring, for 2 minutes. Add the crushed tomatoes with their juice and bring to a boil. Reduce the heat to low, cover, and simmer, stirring occasionally, for 1 hour. Stir in the beans, heat through, and season with salt and pepper. (*Note:* If you prefer your chili to have a "soupier" consistency, add 1 cup water or beef broth at this point and heat through.)

Place the Jack cheese, sour cream, avocado, and cilantro in separate small bowls to use for garnishing. Ladle the chili into warmed individual bowls and serve. Pass the garnishes at table.

tuna, apple, and
your favorite cheese melt

During one summer at the shore, a friend introduced me to the wonders of tuna salad with chopped apples, and it opened my eight-year-old eyes to a new and delicious world of tuna sandwiches. Perhaps it will do the same for your impressionable ones. Let your kids express their preferences and substitute American or Monterey Jack cheese and white bread as they (but really, you) see fit. Involve the kids in the recipe preparation by letting them stir the filling and assemble the sandwiches.

Makes 6 sandwiches

In a small bowl, stir together the mayonnaise, mustard, and lemon juice; reserve.

Preheat a broiler.

In a medium bowl, combine the tuna, apple, celery, and green onions. Add the seasoned mayonnaise and stir gently to mix.

Arrange the bread slices on a broiler pan or baking sheet. Divide the tuna evenly among the bread slices, spreading it evenly, and top each with a slice of the cheese. Slip under the broiler and broil until the cheese melts, 2 to 3 minutes. Serve immediately.

⅓ cup mayonnaise

2 tablespoons Dijon mustard

1 teaspoon fresh lemon juice

2 large cans Albacore tuna, drained

1 small red apple, unpeeled, cored, and finely chopped

2 celery stalks, finely chopped

2 green onions, finely chopped

6 slices rye bread, lightly toasted

6 slices cheese such as Cheddar or Gruyère, each ¼-inch thick

baked macaroni shells
with cheddar cheese

9 tablespoons unsalted butter

salt

1 pound macaroni shells

6 tablespoons all-purpose flour

3 cups whole milk, heated

2½ cups mild or sharp grated
  Cheddar cheese (the orange
  kind, of course)

salt and pepper to taste

1 cup unseasoned fine dried
  bread crumbs

What kid doesn't swoon over macaroni and cheese? In this rendition, I have simply changed the shape of the pasta and ensured that orange Cheddar cheese is used for a Halloween-hued dish. Kids can help measure and mix the ingredients, though I wager they'd rather eat the result.

Serves 6 to 8

Preheat an oven to 350° F. Butter a 2½-quart baking dish, or six to eight 1–1½ cup individual dishes, with 1 tablespoon of the butter.

Bring a large pot of water to a boil and add one or two generous pinches of salt. When the water returns to a boil, add the macaroni. Cook until barely tender, about 10 minutes or according to package directions.

Meanwhile, in a saucepan over medium heat, melt 6 tablespoons of the butter. When the foam begins to subside, whisk in the flour. Cook, whisking constantly, for 2 minutes. *Do not let the flour brown.* Slowly whisk in the hot milk and cook, stirring, until the sauce thickens and boils, about 5 minutes. Add the Cheddar cheese and cook, stirring, until the cheese melts, about 2 minutes longer. Season with salt and pepper.

When the macaroni is ready, drain well and place in a large bowl. Pour the cheese sauce over the macaroni and stir gently to mix. Transfer to the prepared baking dish. Cut the remaining 2 tablespoons butter into bits and use to dot the surface. Sprinkle with the bread crumbs and dot with the remaining butter. Bake, uncovered, until the top is golden brown and the sauce is bubbly, about 30 minutes. Serve at once.

halloween is for adults, too.

When I was a little girl, I felt (and I still do) that my birthday was not long enough for a proper celebration. Why not a birthday weekend, or even a birthday week? The same goes for Halloween, particularly, because 5 years out of 7 it falls on a school (or work) night. Why not extend the festivities to include not only the kids' trick-or-treat night but also a Friday or Saturday evening Halloween dinner party for adults?

Halloween is the perfect adult party theme because it lends itself naturally to spirited fun. Eerie or elegant, free-form or fancy, Halloween lets you express your personal style for this light-hearted occasion.

Assign a theme such as Venetian Masquerade or Hollywood Legends and ask your guests to dress accordingly. Enhance the festivities with music (perhaps the soundtrack from *The Rocky Horror Picture Show* or a Wagner opera). Arrange ivy branches on the table and petite pumpkins and beeswax pillar candles among the ivy leaves. Try piling bright orange persimmons in a black kettle for a naturally beautiful yet eerie effect.

I've created a simple yet stylish Halloween menu that you can prepare and serve without joining the ranks of the living dead. I pair a pork roast—one of the easiest and most impressive main courses for a dinner party—with autumn fruits and vegetables in their own festive guises. It's topped off with an enticing dessert that can be made a day beforehand. Don't forget to serve Halloween candy with the after-dinner coffee!

Autumn Salad with Tangerines, Avocado, and Pumpkin Seeds
Roasted Pork Loin with Quinces and Lady Apples
Mashed Sweet Potatoes with Caramelized Red Onions
Pumpkin Crackle Custard

autumn salad with tangerines, avocado, and pumpkin seeds

A cumin-scented vinaigrette sets off a harmony of flavors and colors in this refreshing autumn salad.

Serves 6

In the bottom of a large salad bowl, combine the vinegar, mustard, cumin, and salt, and whisk to dissolve the salt. Add the olive oil in a slow, steady stream, whisking as you do so. Season with pepper.

Put the lettuce, tangerines, onion, avocado, and pumpkin seeds on top of the dressing in the bowl. If you are not serving the salad immediately, cover it with a damp kitchen towel and refrigerate until ready to serve. If you are serving the salad immediately, toss the greens lightly with the vinaigrette and serve.

For the dressing:

2–3 tablespoons red wine vinegar

1 tablespoon Dijon mustard

¾ teaspoon ground cumin

salt to taste

⅓–½ cup extra-virgin olive oil

ground pepper to taste

2 medium heads red leaf lettuce, leaves separated, carefully rinsed, and dried

2 tangerines, peeled and sectioned

1 red onion, thinly sliced

1 avocado, pitted, peeled, and diced

6 tablespoons roasted pumpkin seeds

roasted pork loin with quinces and lady apples

The beautiful quince, with its creamy yellow skin and its apple-pear shape, is one of autumn's nicest gifts. Due to its coarse texture and astringency, the quince cannot be eaten raw. When cooked, it turns a pale pink and releases its sweet aroma and delicate flavor—an exotic fusion of guava, pineapple, pear, and apple. Baked alongside a pork loin, quinces are pure heaven. If you cannot find Lady apples, substitute quartered Granny Smith apples. And, if you wish, opt only for one or the other fruit and give it star status.

Serves 6 to 8

Place the quince quarters in a saucepan with the grape juice, apple juice, and lemon zest and bring to a boil over medium heat. Reduce the heat to low, cover, and simmer until the quinces are tender, 20 to 30 minutes. Uncover, increase heat to high, and cook until the liquid reduces to about ½ cup, about 5 minutes. Remove from the heat.

Meanwhile, preheat an oven to 450° F. In a small bowl, combine the olive oil, mustard, rosemary, and shallot. Place the pork in a shallow baking dish or roasting pan and spread the olive oil mixture over it. Season with salt and pepper. Roast for 20 minutes.

Remove the roasting pan from oven and arrange the Lady apples around the roast. Return the pan to the oven, reduce the oven temperature to 350° F, and roast for 15 minutes more. Remove the pork from the oven and pour the quince liquid over it. Arrange the quince quarters around the loin, return to the oven, and roast until a meat thermometer inserted into the center of the loin registers 155° F, about 25–35 minutes longer.

Let the meat rest for 15 minutes before slicing. Serve with the fruits and the pan juices.

4 quinces, peeled, quartered, and cored

1½ cups unsweetened white grape juice

1½ cups unsweetened apple juice

1 lemon zest strip, 3 inches long

2 tablespoons olive oil

1 tablespoon Dijon mustard

1 tablespoon finely chopped fresh rosemary

1 tablespoon minced shallot

1 boneless pork loin, 3 pounds

salt and freshly ground pepper to taste

12 Lady apples, unpeeled, left whole and cored through the bottom

mashed sweet potatoes with caramelized red onions

2 tablespoons olive oil

6 tablespoons unsalted butter

1 large red onion, thinly sliced

5 sweet potatoes, peeled and cut into 1-inch chunks

salt to taste

¾ to 1 cup half-and-half, heated

ground pepper to taste

Here sweet potatoes, a staple of autumn cooking, are accented with caramelized red onions. If you have picky eaters, you can eliminate the red onions, but I'd make them anyway as an optional topping for the potatoes.

Serves 6

In a large skillet over medium heat, warm the olive oil with 2 tablespoons of the butter. When the butter melts, add the onion and sauté, stirring occasionally, until golden, about 20 minutes. Using a slotted spoon, transfer the onion to a bowl, cover, and keep warm.

In a large saucepan, combine the sweet potato chunks with water to cover. Bring to a boil over medium-high heat, add a generous pinch of salt, and cook until tender, 10 to 15 minutes.

Drain the sweet potatoes and return to the pan. Shake the pan gently over low heat briefly to evaporate any lingering water. Pass the sweet potatoes through a food mill or ricer placed over a bowl, or mash them in a bowl with a potato masher. Stir in the hot half-and-half, the remaining butter cut into pieces, and the caramelized onions. Season to taste with salt and pepper and serve at once.

pumpkin crackle custard

Children will delight in breaking through the caramelized sugar "crackle" that coats the custard.

Makes 6 servings

In a saucepan over medium heat, combine the cream and star anise. Heat until bubbles form along the edges of the pan. Remove from the heat, cover, and let steep for 30 minutes.

Preheat an oven to 325° F.

Remove the star anise from the cream and discard. Reheat the cream over medium heat just until bubbles form around the edges again. Remove from the heat.

Bring the water to a boil and keep warm. Put the pumpkin puree in a bowl and whisk in the egg yolks. Add ½ cup of the brown sugar and the spices and beat well. Pour ½ cup of the hot cream into the pumpkin mixture, whisking constantly. Add the remaining cream and whisk to combine. Stir in the vanilla.

Ladle the pumpkin custard into six ½-cup ramekins or custard cups, dividing evenly. Transfer them to a baking pan in which they fit snugly but do not touch. Pour in boiling water to reach halfway up the sides of the ramekins. Bake until the custards are set in the center, 25 to 30 minutes. Remove the custards from the water bath and let cool at room temperature for 15 minutes, then cover and refrigerate until cold.

(continued)

1½ cups heavy cream

2 star anise

4 cups water

1 cup unsweetened pumpkin puree (see recipe on page 85)

3 egg yolks

¾ cup light brown sugar

¾ teaspoon ground cinnamon

⅛ teaspoon ground cloves

¼ teaspoon ground allspice

pinch of ground nutmeg

1½ teaspoons pure vanilla extract

Preheat a broiler. Sprinkle a thin layer of the remaining ¼ cup brown sugar evenly over the tops of the custards. Place them 2 to 3 inches under the broiler just until the sugar caramelizes; this will only take 1 to 2 minutes. Serve warm, or chill, uncovered, and serve cold.

halloween crackers

For each Halloween cracker you will need:

one 9-by-12-inch piece of orange or black crepe paper

1 cylindrical cardboard tube, 4½ inches long and 1½ inches in diameter (a toilet tissue tube is ideal)

double-stick tape or craft glue

black and orange pipe cleaners or ribbon

candy and trinkets for filling the crackers

pinking shears (optional)

A novelty from England, Christmas crackers traditionally decorate the holiday table. But why not give them a Halloween outing? I like to fill my Halloween crackers with candy corn and small toys such as rubber spiders and plastic vampire fangs. A mood ring (remember those?) would be a fun addition, too.

Arrange the crepe paper lengthwise on a work surface. Center the cardboard tube on the bottom edge of the paper. Secure the crepe paper to the cardboard tube with a small piece of double-stick tape or craft glue. Roll up the cardboard tube in the crepe paper. Tie one end of the cardboard tube with a pipe cleaner or length of ribbon. Fill the cracker with a few pieces of candy and/or trinkets and tie the other end. Cut the crepe paper ends with pinking shears, if desired.

peek-a-boo place cards

For each place card you will
need:

Construction paper

felt-tip markers

glitter pen (optional)

sequins or wiggle eyes

a cloth or paper napkin

These simple place cards take on eerie personalities when peeking out from a napkin. You might even want to include some candy corn in the pocket!

Trace a Halloween figure such as a witch, owl, or ghost onto construction paper and cut it out. Decorate with markers, glitter pen (if using), and sequins or wiggle eyes. Write the name of your guest on the place card.

To make the pocket napkin, open a napkin flat on a work surface. Fold the top and bottom edges in toward the center. Fold the bottom edge up again so it covers the edges. Evenly fold each long side to the back. Insert your place card in the pocket.

trick-or-treat party favors

For each party favor you will
need:

small cellophane bag

Halloween candy

2-by-1-inch paper tag

⅛-inch-hole paper punch

rick rack, licorice string, or a
    pipe cleaner for tying the bag

Halloween sticker

Let your children determine which tricks will be written on the paper tags and who will be assigned each favor (and trick). Pixies will have fun filling the bags with candy.

Fill the cellophane bag with Halloween candy. Write a trick on the paper tag, such as "jump up and down while rubbing your stomach," or "sing your favorite song." Insert the paper tag in the bag. Punch a hole in the cellophane and thread the rick rack, licorice, or pipe cleaner through it. Tie the bag.

Write your guest's name on the Halloween sticker, and stick it on the bag. Have your guests open their bags after dinner and perform their tricks!

easy illusions

* Gather large cuttings from oak, maple, or birch trees and anchor with sand or rocks in a galvanized bucket against a wall. Attach a clip-on spotlight to the edge of the bucket so it reflects upward. When the light is switched on, the branches will cast eerie shadows on the wall.

* Create a Halloween tree by anchoring a small but full tree branch in an urn. Hang Halloween-themed Christmas ornaments, Flying Ghosts (page 35), or Bats in the Belfry (page 84) on the branches.

* Arrange varying sizes of mercury glass balls along a mantle or dining table. Intersperse with candles.

* Assemble a bouquet of chocolate cosmos, orange Chinese lanterns, and silver dollars. Tie a wide brown satin ribbon around the stems and give the flowers to a friend. Or set the flowers in a pumpkin (insert a glass to hold water) or ceramic pot and enjoy!

* Fill a large urn with baby pumpkins or persimmons and tuck dripless candles in at various angles.

* Arrange grapevines and cuttings along a mantle. Weave tiny, white Christmas lights (tivoli lights) through them. Place persimmons and baby pumpkins and colorful leaves along the garland.

three-tier pumpkin centerpiece

Pumpkins come in all sizes, so they're perfect for stacking into a sculptural centerpiece for the table. Let your imagination guide you. If you like, include winter squashes and root vegetables, too. Be sure the top pumpkin has its stem intact. For real Halloween drama, arrange the centerpiece on a pedestal cake stand. Arrange autumn leaves around the base of each pumpkin.

Arrange the pumpkins on the cake stand or platter with the biggest one on the bottom and smallest one on the top. Tuck autumn leaves and ivy, if using, around the base of the pumpkin sculpture and around the pumpkins in the sculpture, too.

For a centerpiece you will need:

3 pumpkins in descending sizes

pedestal cake stand or platter

selection of colorful autumn leaves, acorns, or dried berries on branches

ivy (optional)

corn kernel napkin rings

If you're doing this with pixies, let them glue the corn kernels on the flat elastic and then sew it for them. Older children can both glue and sew.

Glue the Indian corn or popcorn kernels to the elastic. Let the glue dry. Stitch together the ends of the elastic to form a ring.

For each napkin ring you will need:

clear-drying fabric glue

Indian corn or colored popcorn kernels

1 piece elastic, 6 inches long by 1½ inches wide

sewing needle and thread

spooky sips

Devil's Breath: Kid's Version

For each drink:

Spicy V-8 juice

dash of lime juice

Combine all the ingredients in a glass and stir well. Add ice.

Devil's Breath: Adult's Version

For each drink:

⅔ part Spicy V-8 juice

⅓ part chili pepper–flavored vodka

dash of lime juice

dash of Tabasco sauce

lime zest for garnish

Combine all the ingredients in a shaker with ice and shake to blend. Serve over ice. Garnish with lime zest.

Witch's Kiss: Kid's Version

For each drink:

2 tablespoons cola

1 teaspoon heavy cream

Pour the cola into a small glass such as a cordial glass and carefully pour the heavy cream on top of it. Do not stir; the cream will float on the surface.

Witch's Kiss: Adult's Version

For each drink:

2–4 tablespoons chocolate-flavored liqueur such as Godiva or crème de cacao

1 teaspoon heavy cream

Pour the liqueur into a cordial glass, and carefully pour the cream on top of it. Do not stir; the cream will float on the surface.

halloween excitements

recipes and crafts for sweets and treats

black cat cookies

2 cups unbleached all-purpose
   flour

¼ teaspoon salt

1 teaspoon ground allspice

¼ teaspoon ground nutmeg

10 tablespoons unsalted butter,
   softened

1 cup sugar

1 egg

1½ teaspoons pure vanilla
   extract

For the icing:

2 egg whites

4½ cups confectioners' sugar

1 tablespoon fresh lemon juice

food coloring, black, yellow, and
   pink or red

black licorice strings

These cookies are big black cats that you definitely want in your path. They may look eerie but they make good eating! Kids can help mix the dough, cut out the cookies and then (what fun!) ice them!

Makes about 2 dozen 5- or 6-inch cookies

In a medium bowl, whisk together the flour, salt, allspice, and nutmeg; reserve.

In a large bowl, using an electric mixer set on medium-high speed, beat together the butter and sugar until light and fluffy. Add the egg and vanilla and beat well.

Reduce speed to low, add the flour mixture, and beat until the dough comes together. Turn out the dough onto a lightly floured surface and divide in half. Flatten each half into a disk, wrap separately in plastic wrap, and chill until firm, about 1 hour.

Preheat an oven to 350° F. Line 2 baking sheets with parchment paper.

On a lightly floured surface, roll out the dough ⅛-inch thick. Using a cat-shaped cookie cutter or template 5 or 6 inches in diameter, cut out cookies. Reroll scraps. As you cut the cookies, transfer them to the prepared baking sheets.

Bake until lightly browned on the edges, 8 to 10 minutes. Remove to cooling racks and let cool to room temperature before icing.

To make the icing, place the egg whites in a bowl. Using an electric mixer set on high speed, beat until soft peaks form. Add the confectioners' sugar and lemon juice and continue to beat until thick and shiny. The icing should spread easily. If the icing is too thin, add more sugar; if it's too thick, add a bit of water.

Scoop out half the icing and divide it in half between 2 small bowls. Tint the icing remaining in the large bowl with black food coloring. Tint one of the small bowls with yellow coloring (for the eyes) and the other small bowl with pink or red coloring (for the mouth).

To ice each cookie: spoon black icing onto its center. Smooth with a small spatula or butter knife. Allow to dry for a few minutes. Using a pastry bag with a small plain tip (which works the best) or a small paint brush or toothpicks (if you don't have a pastry bag or the inclination to use one), draw eyes onto the cookie with the yellow icing and a mouth with the pink or red icing. Place 3 licorice strings, cut to fit, on each side of the face for the whiskers.

paper bag pumpkin

Here's a fat and jolly pumpkin to sit on your mantle or table. Pixies will have fun crumpling the newspaper and stuffing the bag. Younger pixies can use their hands to paint the pumpkin; older children can use the paint brushes.

Fill the lunch bag with the crumpled newspaper, filling out the sides so it forms a pumpkin shape. Gather together the top of the bag to form a 1-inch stem. Secure with a rubber band.

Paint the entire bag, except the stem, with the orange paint. Paint the stem green. Use the black paint to paint the features of the jack-o'-lantern.

For each pumpkin you will need:

paper lunch bag,
    preferably white

newspaper, crumpled

rubber band

orange, black, and green
    tempera paints

paint brushes

popcorn balls

2 teaspoons corn oil, plus more
  for greasing your hands

12 cups popped popcorn (¾
  cup unpopped)

1 cup granulated sugar

½ cup brown sugar

1 cup light corn syrup

½ cup water

1 teaspoon fresh lemon juice

½ teaspoon salt

While today popcorn balls are commonly regarded as Christmas treats, they were first made at Halloween by Midwesterners. I say, "Why limit them to any holiday at all?" They're so much fun to make and so wonderful to eat that we ought to whip up a batch any time the popcorn urge hits. Making the syrup should be an adult's job, but kids will get a kick out of forming the popcorn balls.

Makes 12

Arrange 1 or 2 sheets of waxed paper on a work surface. This is your popcorn ball drying area.

Grease a large bowl with the 2 teaspoons corn oil. Put the popped corn in it; reserve. In a saucepan over medium heat, combine all the remaining ingredients. Bring to a boil, stirring frequently. Cook until the syrup reaches 250° F to 260° F on a candy thermometer.

Carefully pour the syrup over the popcorn and toss with a fork to coat the popcorn well. Let cool slightly. Grease your hands with a little corn oil and form the popcorn mixture into 3-inch balls; you should have 12 balls. Place on the waxed paper to cool completely.

Wrap the cooled balls individually in plastic wrap or colored tissue paper. Store in a cool, dry place for up to one week.

old-fashioned fudge

Fudge was one of the first recipes I ever made, and for years I thought evaporated milk was created for this one very important function. Imagine my delight when Marshmallow Fluff, another childhood favorite, threw its hat into the ring. This is a sure kid pleaser ("kid" being a relative descriptor).

Makes about 2½ pounds

Brush a jelly-roll pan with the 1 tablespoon melted butter; reserve.

In a saucepan over medium-low heat, combine the sugar, the 6 tablespoons butter, and the milk. Bring to a boil, stirring to dissolve the sugar. Continue to cook, stirring constantly, for 4 minutes. Remove from the heat and stir in the chocolate, Marshmallow Fluff, salt, and vanilla. Continue to stir until the chocolate melts and the mixture becomes smooth and shiny. Mix in the raisins and walnuts, if using.

Transfer to the prepared jelly-roll pan, spreading evenly. Cover and refrigerate until set, 6 to 8 hours. When the fudge is firm, cut it into squares or use cookie cutters to cut it into Halloween or autumnal shapes. (A tip: to prevent sticking, dip the cookie cutters in cold water between each cutting.)

1 tablespoon unsalted butter, melted, plus 6 tablespoons (¾ stick)

3 cups sugar

1 cup evaporated milk

14 ounces bittersweet or semisweet chocolate, finely chopped

1 cup Marshmallow Fluff

¼ teaspoon salt

1 teaspoon pure vanilla extract

½ cup raisins (optional)

1 cup chopped walnuts, toasted (optional)

caramel apples and pears

12 natural licorice sticks, cinnamon sticks, or bamboo skewers, each 6 inches long

6 Lady apples, stems removed

6 Seckel pears, stems removed

2 cups granola

1 cup sugar

½ cup dark corn syrup

2 teaspoons pure vanilla extract

3 tablespoons water

4 tablespoons (½ stick) unsalted butter

1 cup heavy cream

The petite Lady apples and Seckel pears are just right for making kid-size caramel treats. They're easy to eat, too! If children are helping, they can carefully dip the apples and pears in the caramel and granola. An adult should supervise the fun as hot caramel can burn. I use natural licorice sticks (found in natural foods stores) because they look eerie and they're edible, too. If you can't find licorice sticks, substitute cinnamon sticks or bamboo skewers.

Makes 12

Insert a licorice stick, cinnamon stick, or bamboo skewer into the stem end of each apple and pear. Spread the granola on a baking sheet; reserve. Have ready 1 or more cooling racks or a large sheet of parchment paper for cooling the caramel fruits.

In a saucepan over low heat, combine the sugar, corn syrup, vanilla extract, and water. Cook, stirring, until the sugar melts. Add the butter and cream, raise the heat to medium-high, and bring to a boil. Cook, stirring occasionally, until the caramel registers 240° F on a candy thermometer, about 10 minutes. Remove from the heat and let cool for 2 minutes.

One at a time, dip the apples and pears in the caramel, twirling and swirling them to coat completely. Dip the tops in the granola to coat them, then transfer to the cooling rack or parchment paper to cool. As the apples and pears cool, the caramel will set. Store the caramel apples and pears, wrapped in cellophane if desired, in a cool, dry place until ready to serve or up to 2 days.

jack-o'-lantern cookies

2½ cups unbleached
all-purpose flour

½ teaspoon ground allspice

½ teaspoon ground cinnamon

¼ teaspoon ground ginger

¼ teaspoon ground nutmeg

½ teaspoon baking powder

¼ teaspoon salt

6 tablespoons butter (¾ stick),
softened

½ cup light brown sugar

¼ cup granulated sugar

1 egg yolk, lightly beaten

1 teaspoon pure vanilla extract

½ cup unsweetened pumpkin
puree (see recipe on page 85)

Kids will enjoy stamping out the dough with a pumpkin-shaped cookie cutter, but an adult may want to step in when it comes to carving the jack-o'-lantern's features with a sharp knife. These pumpkin-and-spice-flavored treats are delicious with a cup of cider.

Makes about 4 dozen 3-inch cookies

In a medium bowl, whisk together the flour, allspice, cinnamon, ginger, nutmeg, baking powder, and salt; reserve.

In a large bowl, using an electric mixer set on medium-high speed, beat together the butter, brown sugar, and granulated sugar until light and fluffy. Add the egg yolk and vanilla and beat well. Beat in the pumpkin puree. Reduce the speed to low and add the flour mixture in 3 batches, mixing well after each addition.

Turn out the dough onto a lightly floured surface, divide in half, flatten each half into a disk, wrap separately in plastic wrap, and chill for 30 minutes.

Preheat an oven to 350° F. Line 2 baking sheets with parchment paper.

On a lightly floured surface, roll out 1 of the disks ⅛-inch thick. Using a pumpkin-shaped cookie cutter or cardboard jack-o'-lantern template 5 to 6 inches in diameter, cut out cookies. If using the cookie cutter, finish off the jack-o'-lantern by cutting out eyes and a mouth with the tip of a sharp knife. Repeat with the remaining dough. Transfer the cookies to the prepared baking sheets.

Bake until golden, 12 to 15 minutes. Transfer to a wire rack to cool.

pumpkin pie ice cream

With the help of an ice cream maker, you can transform pumpkin cus-tard into pumpkin pie ice cream in a flash. If you have a bit more time, let the kids churn the ice cream with an old-fashioned manual ice cream maker—a fun activity for a Halloween or autumn birthday party.

Makes 1½ quarts

In a saucepan over medium heat, combine the half-and-half and heavy cream. Heat until small bubbles appear along the edges of the pan.

Meanwhile, in a bowl, whisk together the egg yolks, sugar, maple syrup, and spices until thick and smooth, 3 to 4 minutes. Pour ½ cup of the hot cream into the egg mixture, whisking as you do. While whisk-ing constantly, slowly pour the egg mixture into the hot milk, then cook over medium-low heat until the custard thickens and leaves a trail on the back of a wooden spoon when a finger is drawn through it, about 6 minutes. Remove from the heat and let cool to room tempera-ture. Stir in the pumpkin puree and crystallized ginger, cover, and chill for 1 hour.

Pour the mixture into an ice cream maker and freeze according to the manufacturer's directions.

2 cups half-and-half

2 cups heavy cream

5 egg yolks

¾ cup light brown sugar

2 tablespoons maple syrup

½ teaspoon ground cinnamon

½ teaspoon ground allspice

¼ teaspoon ground nutmeg

¼ teaspoon ground ginger

4 cups unsweetened pumpkin puree (see recipe on page 85)

¼ cup chopped crystallized ginger

cocoa cobweb cupcakes

Follow this fun technique for creating cobwebs with two different colors of frosting. You can do this on cookies and cakes, too. Kids can line the muffin tins, mix the ingredients, spoon the batter into the muffin cups and of course, supervise the icing.

Makes 12 cupcakes

Preheat an oven to 350° F. Butter 12 muffin-tin wells or line them with paper muffin cups.

In a medium bowl, whisk together the flour, cocoa, baking powder, baking soda, and salt; reserve.

In a large bowl, using an electric mixer set on medium-high speed, beat together the butter and sugar until light and fluffy. Add the egg and vanilla and beat well. Beat in the flour mixture in 3 batches, alternately with the buttermilk.

Spoon into the prepared muffin tins, filling each cup about two-thirds full. Bake until a toothpick inserted in the center of the cake comes out clean, 16 to 20 minutes. Remove from the oven, let cool in the pan for 5 minutes, then transfer to a rack and let cool to room temperature.

To make the icing, place the egg whites in a bowl. Using an electric mixer set on high speed, beat until soft peaks form. Add the confectioners' sugar, vanilla, and orange juice and continue to beat until thick and shiny. The icing should spread easily. If too thick, add more orange juice. If too thin, add more confectioners' sugar.

(continued)

2 cups unbleached all-purpose flour

3 tablespoons unsweetened cocoa, preferably Dutch-process

1 teaspoon baking powder

½ teaspoon baking soda

¼ teaspoon salt

4 tablespoons (½ stick) unsalted butter, softened

1½ cups sugar

1 egg

2 teaspoons pure vanilla extract

1 cup buttermilk

For the icing:

2 egg whites

2½ to 3 cups confectioners' sugar

1 teaspoon pure vanilla extract

2 tablespoons fresh orange juice

black or dark brown food coloring

Transfer one-third of the icing to a small bowl and color with black or dark brown food coloring. Spoon this dark icing into a pastry bag fitted with a tip, or pour it into a plastic squeeze bottle.

Now, ice the cupcakes and make the cobwebs: Spoon the white icing into the center of the cupcake and spread with a small spatula or butter knife. Starting at the center of a cupcake, pipe a spiral of the dark icing from the center to the outer edge. Then, drag a sharp knife point from the center of the spiral to the edge of the cupcake. Wipe the knife clean, move about a ½ inch to the left or right and drag the knife in the opposite direction from the outer edge to the middle of the cupcake. Continue in this way until you have worked your way around the cupcake and formed the cobweb. Repeat with the remaining cupcakes.

bats in the belfry

For each bat you will need:

spring-loaded clothespin

black tempera paint

pencil

black construction paper

glue

sequins or wiggle eyes

These delightful, frightful bats are created from clothespins and black tempera paint. Clip them onto curtains, and they'll guard your home from Halloween spirits. Clasp them onto your jacket, and you'll be safe from goblins on Halloween night. Pixies can paint the clothespins and glue the wings, but they may need help tracing the bat wings and cutting them out.

Paint the clothespin black and let dry. Using the pencil, draw 3-inch bat wings on the black construction paper. Cut out the wings from the construction paper. Glue the wings onto the clothespin, covering the spring. For the head, glue sequins or wiggle eyes on the clothespin "pincher."

how to make fresh pumpkin puree

I like to roast the pumpkin for pureeing because the oven heat draws out the pumpkin's earthy, sweet flavor, and unlike boiling, the pumpkin does not become waterlogged. While using canned pumpkin is more convenient, you might want to experience the flavor of fresh puree. This is also a great way to show your kids where the canned stuff comes from. Use fresh pumpkin puree whenever a recipe calls for unsweetened pumpkin puree.

1 tablespoon vegetable oil

1 pumpkin such as Jack Be Little, Munchkin, or Spookie, 2 pounds

Makes 2 cups

Preheat an oven to 400° F. Brush a baking sheet with the oil.

Cut the pumpkin in half horizontally and scoop out the seeds and strings (save the seeds for roasting, page 18). Place the pumpkin halves cut sides down on the prepared baking sheet. Bake until the flesh is soft when pierced with a fork, 45 to 60 minutes. Remove from the oven and let cool.

Scoop out the flesh into a food processor or blender. Puree until smooth. Spoon the pumpkin puree into a sieve placed over a large bowl. Let the pumpkin drain for 30 minutes before using. Cover and refrigerate for up to 1 week, or freeze up to 1 year.

jiggle pumpkins and wiggle bats

1 box orange Jell-O

1 box blackberry or grape Jell-O

Pearl B. Wait, who introduced Jell-O to the American public in 1897, must have been a fun person. Not only do these pumpkins and bats jiggle and wiggle, they're fruity-good, too. Your kids will have a blast making and eating these, and I dare say, should you have the gumption to serve them at a dinner party, your guests will go batty (sorry!) for them, too.

Lightly spray 2 shallow pans, such as jelly roll pans, with nonstick cooking spray.

Prepare the boxes of Jell-O according to the package directions. Pour each into a prepared pan and chill until set.

Using cookie cutters, cut pumpkins from the orange Jell-O and bats from the purple Jell-O. Eat!

handprint ghosts

For each ghost you will need:

White construction paper

Black magic marker or wiggle eyes

craft glue (if using wiggle eyes)

Remember those handprint Thanksgiving turkeys we made in grammar school—our palm for the body, thumb for its head, and fingers for its feathers? These handprint ghosts turn that turkey on its head! In this fast and fun project, the body of the turkey becomes the head of the ghost, and the feathers and head form its flowing bottom. The handprint ghosts make fun place cards or name tags, as well as an eerily cute Halloween greeting.

Trace your hand on a sheet of paper and turn it upside down. Draw a half circle at the top to join the two lines where your wrist was. Draw eyes, or glue wiggle eyes, on the head, and draw a big O for the mouth. Cut out the ghost. If you like, you can write a note on the back.

devil's food cake

2 cups cake flour

1 teaspoon baking soda

½ teaspoon salt

8 ounces bittersweet or semisweet chocolate, chopped

1¾ cups sugar

1¼ cups buttermilk

½ cup (1 stick) unsalted
butter, softened

3 eggs

1 egg yolk

1½ teaspoons pure vanilla
extract

For the frosting:

4 tablespoons unsalted butter,
softened

¼ cup light brown sugar

¼ cup pure maple syrup

2 egg whites

1¼ cup confectioners' sugar

milk, if needed, to thin

I think this cake is called devil's food because it's sinfully simple and good. If Halloween doesn't give you an excuse to dig in, no other holiday will. The cake forms an appealing crust and a tender texture when it bakes, and is wonderful even without frosting. Your children, however, will demand the gooey stuff, so I have obliged with a recipe for maple frosting. This is black magic at its tastiest.

Makes one 9-inch layer cake; serves 8 to 10

Preheat an oven to 350° F. Butter and flour two 8- or 9-inch cake pans, tapping out the excess flour.

In a small bowl, whisk together the cake flour, baking soda, and salt; reserve.

In a small saucepan over low heat, combine the chocolate, ½ cup of the sugar, and ½ cup of the buttermilk. Cook, stirring, until the chocolate melts and the mixture is smooth, about 5 minutes. Remove from the heat and let cool 5 minutes.

In a large bowl, using an electric mixer set on medium-high speed, beat together the butter and the remaining 1¼ cups sugar until light and fluffy. Add the eggs and egg yolk one at a time, beating well after each addition. Beat in the vanilla. Reduce the speed to low and add the flour mixture in 3 batches alternately with the remaining ¾ cup buttermilk. Stir in the chocolate mixture until well blended. Pour the batter into the prepared pans, dividing evenly. Bake until the cakes begin to pull away from the sides of the pan and a toothpick inserted into the center comes out clean, 30 to 40 minutes. Remove from the oven and let cool in the pans for 10 minutes. Turn the cakes out onto cooling racks and let cool to room temperature.

To make the frosting, in a bowl, using an electric mixer set on medium-high speed, beat together the butter, brown sugar, and maple syrup until light and fluffy. In a separate bowl, using clean, dry beaters, beat the egg whites on medium speed until foamy. Sift the confectioners' sugar over the egg whites and beat on high speed until stiff peaks form. Using a rubber spatula, fold the egg whites into the butter mixture until well mixed. If you desire a thinner frosting, add a bit of milk. If you desire a thicker frosting, add more confectioners' sugar. You should have about 1½ cups frosting.

To frost the cake, place a layer upside down on a serving plate, so the flatter side is facing up. Spread frosting over the surface of the layer. Carefully place the remaining layer, flatter side down, directly on top of it. Using an icing spatula or a wide knife, spread a thin layer of frosting, called a crumb coat, over the sides of the cake. Now top this thin coating with a thicker layer of frosting. Spoon the remaining frosting onto the center of the top layer and spread it out toward the edges. Using the back of a spoon, make swirl decorations on the tops and sides.

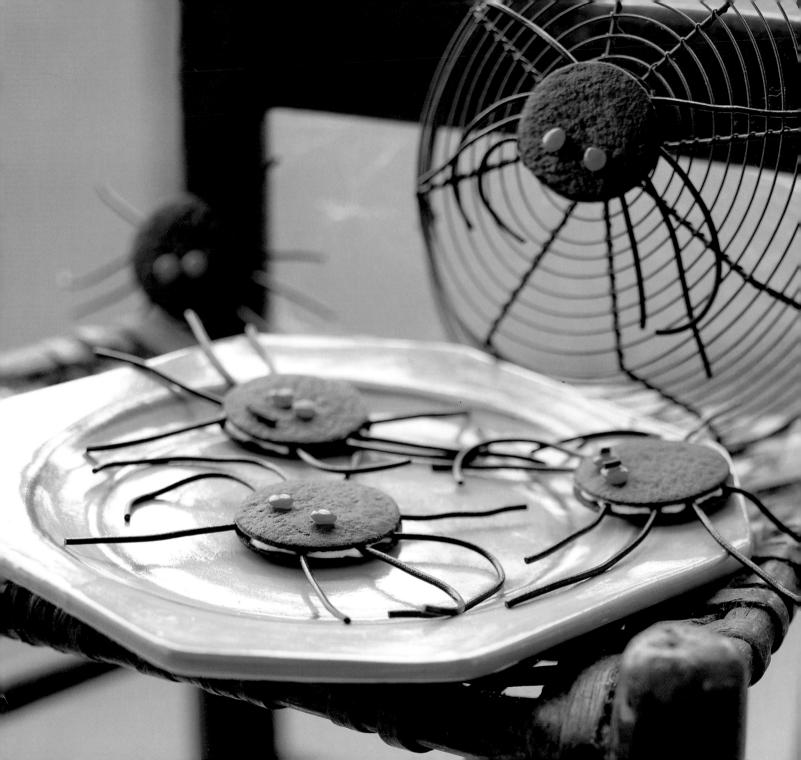

sweetie spiders

You'll want to make friends with these spiders. They're scarily sweet!

Makes 12

In a small bowl, stir together the confectioners' sugar and enough water—3 to 4 drops—to form a thick paste; reserve.

Cut the licorice strings in half. Stick 4 halves into the cream on each side of the cookie to form the legs. Using the confectioners' sugar paste as glue, adhere two cinnamon candies on the top of the cookie to form the eyes. Eat—if you dare!

2 tablespoons confectioners' sugar

a few drops of water

48 thin black licorice strings, each 6 inches long

12 chocolate cream sandwich cookies

24 small red cinnamon candies such as Red-Hots

black rock spider

These spiders make fun party favors or paperweights. Pixies can choose the rocks at the nursery (or search for them outdoors), and glue the legs and eyes.

Cut the pipe cleaners in half. Glue 4 pipe cleaner halves onto each side of the rock's underside to form the legs. Accordion-fold the legs to form the joints. Glue on the sequins or wiggle eyes.

For each spider you will need:

1 smooth, rounded landscape rock, available at nurseries

4 black pipe cleaners

sequins or wiggle eyes

craft glue

shrunken heads

For each head you will need:

1 large Red Delicious apple, firm and not overly ripe

potato peeler or small sharp knife

¼ cup lemon juice

small paintbrush

1 tablespoon kosher salt

2 whole cloves

It's fun to watch the features emerge as the apple head dries and shrinks over the course of a week or two.

Preheat an oven to 100° F (or the lowest setting on the dial).

Peel the apple. Using the potato peeler or knife, carve eyes, a nose, and a mouth by cutting about ¼ inch into the apple. Brush the lemon juice over the entire surface of the apple and then rub the entire surface with the salt.

Stick in the two cloves for the eyes. Dry the apple in the oven for 2 hours, then transfer to a drying rack and let the apple dry in a warm place for 1 to 2 weeks. The facial features will become more prominent as the face shrinks.

creature cut-ups

Paper dolls take on scary flair when they become creature cut-ups. Instead of construction paper, use leftover gift wrap if you want your creatures to be elegant or funny, but be sure to glue two pieces of gift wrap together so you have designs on both sides. Tissue paper is fun to use, too! Younger pixies will need assistance with cutting out the creatures, but they can decorate the finished line-up with crayons, markers, or paint.

Fold the paper into four or more equal sections. On the top section, draw a Halloween creature such as a ghost or bat. Make sure that the drawing touches the folds on both sides in at least one place.

Cut out the design, being careful not to cut in those places where the drawing touches the edges.

If you wish, decorate the cut-ups with the crayons, markers, or paint.

Hang the creature cut-ups in doorways, or string them along a mantle or tabletop.

For each cut-up you will need:

1 sheet of construction paper (any color), 12 inches square

scissors

crayons, felt-tip markers, or tempera or watercolor paint (optional)

invisible ink art

On Halloween night, spirits leave secret messages. Write the message for your child to read on Halloween night, or help him or her to create messages and pictures to share with family and friends.

With the paintbrush or your finger, use apple juice or milk to paint a picture or a message on the paper. Let dry completely.

To see the invisible picture or read the message, carefully hold the paper near a hot incandescent light bulb.

You will need:

small paintbrush (optional)

apple juice or milk

white paper (such as typing paper or notebook paper)

stained-glass spooks

Halloween cookie cutters such as pumpkin, ghost, cat, and bat

heavy-duty aluminum foil

canola or safflower oil

small hard candies in assorted colors, such as Jolly Ranchers (the best) or LifeSavers

wooden skewer

satin baby ribbon, ⅛-inch wide

These stained-glass creatures can be hung in a window to catch sunlight or moonlight. Here's a secret: you can eat them, too!

Preheat an oven to 350° F.

Line the bottom and interior sides of the cookie cutters with aluminum foil and brush the foil lightly with the oil. Set on a baking sheet.

Arrange the hard candies in a single layer on the foil bottom of the cookie cutter. Bake until the candies melt, about 10 minutes.

Remove from the oven, let cool for 1 minute, then poke a hole in the top with the wooden skewer. Cool; then pop out the stained glass shapes from the cookie cutter and peel off the aluminum foil. Thread the ribbon through the hole. Hang in a sunny window.

index